GLIMPSES OF GOD

A Guided Personal Retreat

Richard Stoltz

Table of Contents

Foreword

Listen.

Do you hear the silence? I firmly believe that only in that stillness can we come to recognize, listen to, and embrace the voice of God. When our life gets so noisy and busy that there is no time or space for stillness, we begin to feel exhausted and drained. Often, we begin to feel alienated from the world and the people around us. No one seems to understand us or our needs. We feel even God has begun to ignore us. In all of that busy noise which we have let creep into our lives, we often don't understand our own self—truly not recognizing our own needs. For this reason many people turn from the busyness of our lives to a quiet retreat to try to listen to our own hearts, and, in doing so, trying to hear again the voice of God.

Richard Stoltz was there to gently lead many of us into the stillness, to guide us back to our heart, and to stay beside us as once again we began to recognize God's voice.

Richard was an educator, psychotherapist, and seasoned spiritual director with degrees in theology, spirituality, physics and counseling. He was a Jesuit for more than thirty years preaching and directing retreats throughout the country. But, far more importantly, he recognized so clearly the voice of God in his life, heard in the gentleness of silence and lived in the joy of loving and being loved. He lived that love both in the Sacrament of Holy Orders and, later, in the Sacrament of Matrimony.

I know. I had the privilege of being his and his wife Maureen's pastor for the last twenty-five years of Richard's life. I saw Christ's healing power embrace those who had come to Richard because they were confused, frightened, or experienced life as out of control. I saw peace and understanding—insight and inspiration—envelop those who attended his retreats. I experienced for myself personal renewal, sound wisdom and loving comfort from one whose soul reflected so beautifully Christ's gentle presence. And I watched as he accepted his terminal illness with the peace of one who knows God and trusts in His love—even until one's last breath.

Richard's step-by-step guide can prepare you to meet God head-on in the powerful experience of Holy Peaceful Quiet. Through Richard's writings, you can benefit from the wisdom and experience of one whose intimacy with God was reflected in his loving and compassionate presence with others. We can benefit from a guiding presence of one who knows the path because, in Christ, he walked it. And, we can benefit from the spirituality and humanness of a man who not only taught us how to live but also how to die.

Listen.

Do you hear the silence?

Monsignor Patrick Bishop
Retired Pastor
Transfiguration Catholic Church,
Marietta, Georgia

This book is dedicated in loving memory to its author,
Richard Stoltz

Richard finished writing his book shortly before being
diagnosed with pancreatic cancer, and went home to God
three weeks later.

I promised him that his book would be published.
Here it is.

Net proceeds from the sale of this book
will be donated for pancreatic cancer research.

Maureen Hunt
Waynesville, North Carolina
November 2015

Introduction

The idea for this book came from people who made retreats at Ignatius House Retreat Center in Atlanta, Georgia, and who, after attending retreats at which I preached, asked me for copies of any materials or copies of tapes they could listen to. That the question kept arising and that some Jesuit friends had been encouraging me for years to write a book on the subject (I kept saying to myself, "*What would I write?*") got me into motion to do something about it. This book is the outcome of my experience and those requests.

I imagine the people who would find this material interesting and helpful are Christians interested in making a quiet retreat on their own and who would like some help directing their prayer, or Christians who simply find "spiritual reading" a help in their daily prayer lives. Most people who make retreats at Ignatius House are Catholic Christians, so the implicitly Catholic orientation of what I have to say to them goes down easily. On the other hand, I haven't heard any complaints from those of other denominations who have made the retreats, so I have (perhaps, naively) assumed that this approach passes muster for them also—and I hope that it will do the same for you.

This little work is divided into chapters that roughly correspond to the talks I've given on retreats. They are intended to help you to get your "inner motor" running, so that afterwards you can spend time in prayer with the Lord and open yourself to what he wants to do in you. This dynamic—to take in some aids to prayer and then pray yourself using what you've taken in or follow the Spirit's lead in entirely different directions—is designed to emphasize the time you spend with the Lord rather than the content or cleverness of the material presented.

In his brief book, *The Spiritual Exercises,* St Ignatius Loyola emphasizes the overwhelming importance of the Creator dealing freely and directly with the individual, and as such, the guidance is designed as assistance to get the two of you closer together and free conversation. Anyone familiar with *The Spiritual Exercises* of St Ignatius Loyola will recognize some of the structure of his exercises in the chapters in this book and that they simply represent my take on the exercises as they can be relevant to our society, and condensed into a brief time. I apologize to Ignatius for any possible and unintentional distortions of his teachings.

Beginning with Chapter Two, *Getting in the Boat,* each chapter in this book includes some suggestions for making a retreat as well as a meditation on the subject material, and Scripture references which are on the same theme as the meditation and which may provide further stepping-off points for your prayer. For some, the suggestions will be unnecessary, so feel free to skip over them and get right to the heart of the matter, the meditation.

If you want to use these reflections to make a retreat for yourself, you can do it in any creative way that works for you. Some people will be able to set aside a weekend at home or away where they can have a bit of quiet time to hear what the Lord is saying to them at this time in their lives. If during this time you can pull off not having to talk, to watch TV or to work on the computer or any digital device, this would be the ideal situation. But do recognize that not everyone who yearns for time like this can make it happen, so be flexible and adjust your setting and available time to fit what works in your life. Try not to let "could be better" get in the way of "good enough." On the other hand, if you can, make your retreat a weeklong experience, not just a weekend. You get the idea. Simply use your creativity to make happen what YOU need and don't get caught by some ideal of having to do it "right." (More on doing it "right" later.)

A Note about the Scripture Passages in this Book

All Scripture passages included herein are taken from *The New American Bible, Revised Edition* ©2010, 1991 1986, 1970, Confraternity of Christian Doctrine Washington, D.C., and are used by permission of the copyright owner. All Rights Reserved. No part of *The New American Bible* may be reproduced in any form without permission in writing from the copyright owner.

Chapter One:
Starting a Retreat

A retreat is about experience. Not necessarily about getting your thinking straight or getting your life in order, although either or both of those can happen because of the retreat experience. We can, for example, have profound experiences that move our souls but don't change our lives. I once watched a symphony orchestra perform Beethoven's *Symphony No. 5 in E Minor* and the experience of listening to the incredible music and watching the musicians put their hearts into it moved me to tears. But I didn't walk out of the auditorium a changed man, nor did I take any action that before the experience I was unable to take. Profound as it was, it was purely an aesthetic experience.

On the other hand, when I have had a religious experience, I might be moved to my soul but not only do I experience that I have been touched, I know I've been touched by Ultimate Power, so that I find myself changed in my feelings, thoughts, and energy to be able to do things I could not have done before. For me, the "proof of the pudding" lies in the doing. I find myself able to do what before I could not do. These new abilities, or changes, might involve forgiving someone who has offended me, putting a regimen of prayer into my life, longing for God, or being able to be at peace within myself and with the world.

Why do we need a retreat to experience this? We don't. However, when we are able to quiet down our lives for a time, practice spiritual exercise, and do what we can to listen, our experiences of God are usually deeper and more moving than

4

those in our daily life. The quiet of a retreat is about *listening*, not about refraining from speaking.

A retreat is not the time to give yourself lectures on what you should be doing in your life. The problem with giving lectures to yourself is that what you hear is the same inner voice you have been hearing for years, saying the same things, and not giving you the ability to take action on those things. Carl Jung said that when we go inside ourselves and quiet down some of the outside noise, the first voice we hear is that of our Inner Critic. To put it simply, the Inner Critic tells us how we're failing (and that's a good thing) but it doesn't give us the grace (or ability or capability) to do anything different.

Chapter Two:
Getting in the Boat

When I start a retreat I usually have a mixture of feelings: anticipation, excitement, fear, uncertainty. Some of the questions that buzz around in my mind are ones like these: What does the Lord have in store for me during this time? What if I don't do it right? What if I get bored? What if I'm here but the Lord doesn't show up? What if I sleep the entire time?

When I finally arrive at my retreat I usually come to it trailing dozens of clouds of concern behind me. I'm still dealing with all the things I had to get in place to have some quiet time: Did I arrange meals for the family? Did I return the phone calls I promised to make? Did I turn off the stove? And so on. I find that it takes a while for these clouds to clear, for all of me to arrive, for my mind to quiet down and for my body to relax.

As you begin a retreat I encourage you to let your busy mind and tired body gradually wind down. You've made whatever arrangements you could. Let that be enough!

Please be gentle with yourself. The kind of insights and changes you seek happen much better in an atmosphere of gentleness than in one of dogged determination. One of my favorite images for starting a retreat is that of Jesus inviting his disciples to come away for a picnic. You remember the scene (Mark 6.30-34).

Jesus has been teaching huge crowds of people and he and his disciples are exhausted, so he tells them, "Let's get away for a bit and cross the Sea of Galilee." He recognizes his and their need for getting away from it all for a while.

Get in the boat and join them. In your imagination hear yourself being invited by Jesus and see yourself in the boat with the other fishermen. Watch the busy shoreline gradually recede into the distance and let it represent the cares and concerns you have right now. Moving away from that shoreline is not being irresponsible; it's necessary in order to let the Lord give you perspective. The astronauts on their early space missions were struck by the littleness of their concerns when they could see the entire earth from a distance. It was a life-changing experience for them all.

Do you have an agenda for your retreat? A question you want answered or a decision you need to make? I suggest asking the Lord right at the beginning of the retreat for what you want and then putting it in his hands rather than focusing your attention on it. Often the Lord's solutions to our problems are much larger than what we wanted to get. A friend told me his pastor says, "When you ask God for something he gives one of three answers: yes, not now, or here's something better." Frequently answer number three happens to people making a retreat. What you want may be too small and the Lord answers you with something more marvelous than what you dare ask for and his answer includes the thing you want.

I suggest you look at this beginning of a retreat from God's point of view. First, it was God's idea, not yours. The idea of making a retreat came to you; you didn't invent it yourself. Perhaps someone told you about retreats, or maybe you've made retreats before and something within you said, "It's time for another retreat"; or maybe you came across this book and said, "Why not?"

Whatever your perceived reason and wherever you are, you are here by his invitation. And you wouldn't have been invited if there weren't something wonderful in store for you. God says (Isaiah 55.11), "My word goes forth and doesn't return to me without doing what I sent it to do." Since the Lord is the host and you're the guest, expect him to have prepared a good time for you.

I'm going to suggest a few thoughts and some passages from Scripture that you may want to consider as you relax into some quiet time.

Jesus saying, "Come to me all you who labor and are overburdened, and I will give you rest" (Matthew 11.28) is good for Americans, who tend to feel vaguely guilty whenever we're not being "productive." Listen. You have Jesus' own word on it. It's okay to "waste time" with him. Think of some of the invitations God has issued to his people in Scripture. In Exodus 3.1-5 we read:

"Meanwhile Moses was tending the flock of his father-in-law Jethro, the priest of Midian. Leading the flock beyond the wilderness, he came to the mountain of God, Horeb. There the angel of the Lord appeared to him as fire flaming out of a bush. When he looked, although the bush was on fire, it was not being consumed. So Moses decided, 'I must turn aside to look at this remarkable sight. Why does the bush not burn up?' When the Lord saw that he had turned aside to look, God called out to him from the bush: Moses! Moses! He answered, 'Here I am.' God said: 'Do not come near! Remove your sandals from your feet, for the place where you stand is holy ground."

This was the call to Moses from the burning bush in which God invited him to take off his shoes for this is a holy place. What's the feel of taking off your shoes? Usually we feel more natural, less defended, maybe more vulnerable. I sometimes take off my shoes when I pray this scene because it makes me feel more grounded, earthier, and more in touch with my humanity and with who I am. You don't take off your shoes if you intend to get along down the road. When you're on holy ground, you can relax and be yourself. You're safe on holy ground!

One other image to consider comes from Isaiah 55.1-12.

"All you who are thirsty, come to the water!
    You who have no money, come, buy grain and eat;
Come buy grain without money, wine and milk without cost!

Why spend your money for what is not bread;
    your wages for what does not satisfy?
Only listen to me, and you shall eat well,
    you shall delight in rich fare."

This is a great passage for any of you who, like me, have to do everything the "right way." Try to remember that no matter how well or poorly you "do it," the Lord will be there for you. No matter if you can't pray the "right way," the Lord will be there for you. No matter if your prayer is full of distractions, God will be present. The great psychotherapist Carl Jung had the following phrase inscribed over the door of a tower he built for his own quiet time: *Aut vocatus aut non vocatus aderit Deus* ("Whether called or not called God will be present.").

A retreat is a wonderful time to relax and be just who you are and sometimes to rediscover who you are. The experience of relaxing into the Lord is often one of coming to something new and yet also very familiar.

If it appeals to you, you might want to let one of the images linger in your imagination: Let Jesus invite you and the other disciples to get away from it all and cross the sea for a picnic. Go with Moses and let the Lord tell you to take off your shoes. God sends his word upon the earth like the rain, which comes down from the heavens and doesn't go back into the sky without watering the soil and letting the crops grow and his people drink. Imagine coming to the water and getting food to eat without having the right price. However quiet happens for you, quiet down and let the Lord come to you his way. It will be much better than your way.

Scripture References
Isaiah 55.11   My word does what I sent it to do
Mark 6.30-33   The picnic by the lake
Matthew 11.28   Come to me
Exodus 3.1-6   Take off your shoes
Isaiah 55.1-2   Come to the water
Philippians 1.6 God will complete the work he has
                 begun in you

Chapter Three:
We're Made for Happiness

During your retreat, don't try to pray all the time. Pray when you have set aside time for prayer and relax or get some exercise (walking seems to help) between prayer times. These breaks can help keep your prayer from becoming too diffuse and unfocused. If you're making this a week-long retreat, notice that some of the things you pray about during your set-aside prayer time will often lead to new perspectives, new insights, or new abilities in your daily life.

Make notes. After you spend some time in prayer, jot down a few notes on what happened, but don't (if you can avoid it) analyze your prayer while it's going on. That's like making love and checking to see how well you're doing it at the same time. Analyzing pulls you out of the experience and takes you into your head. (Some of us are so aware of what we're doing that it's like being onstage all the time. If that sounds like you, let it be a little joke between you and God. Pray something like, "All right, Father, here I am, you know, the one who watches myself all the time; otherwise, You might wonder who this is.") The notes you write can help after the retreat when you may wonder, "Did that really happen to me?" and they can help you see a pattern in what's happening between God and you during this time.

God made us to be happy! It's so hard for us to hold onto that fact. It's very difficult for us to get past a deep-set belief that we aren't okay just as we are. The immediate result of Adam and Eve's sin was their feeling that they weren't okay as they were. They began to cover their nakedness because they were ashamed, not of what they had done, but ashamed of their very selves. But more on that later.

Let's get something straight from the beginning: Not only does God love you, God is "in love" with you. Sometimes doing marriage counseling I have heard one or the other partner say that they genuinely loved his or her spouse, but were never "in love" with them. This "in love" statement refers to a time when the other occupied your every thought, when every event was seen through the eyes of your loved one, when to be deprived of the other's presence was so painful it almost physically hurt.

The Scriptures are full of love letters from God to us, his own. "Before I formed you in the womb I knew you, and before you were born I consecrated you." (Jeremiah 1.5) And they are full of the assertion that God loved us first and that's why he made us. It's easy to see how much the Father loved Jesus, calling him his beloved son, working powerfully through him and affirming how pleased he is with Jesus. When Jesus hears the Father say at his baptism, "You are my beloved son, in you I am well pleased," (Mark 1.11) I don't think the Father is saying, "Jesus, you're doing a good job, and therefore you're my beloved son." It's not like he's giving Jesus his mid-term grade. It's more like Jesus is his own, his only begotten son and he loves him. As the Father looks at you, he sees his own child who was loved into existence. So the Father is able to look at you now and say, "This is my beloved daughter or son, in whom I am well pleased."

Some people have tried to express it this way: "When the Father looks at us, he sees Jesus." Jesus says to you, "As the Father has loved me so I have loved you." He loves you that much! These are difficult sayings for those of us who have learned to earn our value to parents, society, churches, employers, and perhaps even to spouses. Discovering that someone loves you just as you are can be a shocking experience and sometimes an experience that takes a lifetime to absorb.

In Isaiah 49.15 God says:

"Can a mother forget her infant,
  be without tenderness for the child of her womb?
Even should she forget,
  I will never forget you.
See, upon the palms of my hands I have engraved you."

Each time God looks at his hands he sees you there. You are never out of his mind. And isn't it interesting that God is seeing a wounded hand when he looks at us?

In Psalm 139.13-18 the Psalmist says to God:

"You formed my inmost being;
  you knit me in my mother's womb.
I praise you, because I am wonderfully made;
  wonderful are your works!
My very self you know.
  My bones are not hidden from you,
When I was being made in secret,
  fashioned in the depths of the earth.
Your eyes saw me unformed;
  in your book all are written down,
my days were shaped, before one came to be.
  How precious to me are your designs, O God;
how vast the sum of them!
  Were I to count them, they would outnumber the sands;
when I complete them, still you are with me."

Notice that the theme isn't just, "God made me." It only starts then. The psalmist is aware that God is still with him, thinking so many thoughts about him that they are as uncountable as the grains of sand. God made you because he loves you and he keeps you in existence by continuing to love you. Creation is not just a one-time event in our past. We are sustained in existence by the Father's steadfast love. It's not only a temporal thing that your coming to be depends on God; it's a psychological issue as well. I can't be thoroughly myself without being known by God. I need God to know me through and through in order to be at peace with myself. Then when I know how deeply I'm known, to discover how equally deeply I'm loved makes me whole.

Walk outside, and let the world around you speak to you. Use your senses and allow yourself to see what's there. This is different from looking around and thinking what's there. Look at the barrenness or the lushness of the trees, the blue or grey of the sky, the texture of the bark on the trees, the flitting of a bird or the waving of grass in the breeze. Let yourself just take it in. Do the same for what you hear. Listen to the sounds around you, to traffic or children shouting, to the rustle of the wind in the trees, to the sound of a bird's call. Spend some time touching, smelling. Let your senses do what they are good at—taking in the entire world around you.

If that puts you in touch with God, just stay with those experiences. Just "Be still and know that I am God." Or, in a more accurate translation, "Be still and know that I am." In fact, "I am" is the name God gives himself when Moses asks, "Who shall I say sent me?"

Or, you may want to reflect quietly on what you are experiencing. All this goes on without any effort on your part; it all works and continues to work even without a plan of ours. And it goes on without any attention or permission on your part. It's simply available to you whenever you turn your attention to it.

Nature is deeply healing and some of what it heals is our illusion that *we* make everything happen, that without our work nothing would go on. It's easy to believe that illusion because so much in our lives requires planning and attention from us. But the most important things don't work that way. We aren't responsible for our vision, hearing or other senses. They're simply there for us. We don't have to make the world of nature— it just is. We don't have to make bread nourish us or water slake our thirst, or a child's voice delight our ears and touch our hearts. Not only are the best things in life free, the most important things are just given.

You, yourself, are not responsible for your coming to be, or your continuing to be. That's simply given to you and you respond to it. I'm not saying that we have nothing to do or that we have no responsibility for what happens to us, only that our freedom is exercised within the context of what is already provided for us, that our job as humans is to respond to the invitations that are constantly being issued to us by God.

You're very aware of all you have to do. I'm inviting you to pay attention to the part that you don't. To attend to the quiet voice of God within you, like Ezekiel who didn't find the Lord in the thunder, the earthquake, the fire, but in a still, quiet voice.

When you look at your world from the point of view of what is given rather than what you do, you will find your heart touched by the love and generosity of the God who keeps doing all these things for you.

So I encourage you: Be with God as you can, not as you can't. Pray as you can, not as you can't. Know that who you are and how you are right now is all God needs to touch your heart and give you the blessings he so much desires to give you today. And no matter how well or poorly you do this, God will give you exactly what you need right now.

Scripture References

Jeremiah 1.4-5   I knew you before you were born
Isaiah 49.15-16   Can a mother forget her child?
Psalm 139   You knit me together in my mother's womb
Exodus 3.13-14   'I am' has sent me to you
1 Kings 19.11-13 God in the tiny voice/breeze

Chapter Four:
Is That You God?

In a movie about Joan of Arc, one of her judges asks Joan why she's out on the battlefield leading armies and she replies that God told her to. The judge says something like, "Come on, Joanie, aren't you confusing the voice of God with your imagination?" To which she replies "Well, if God can't speak to us through our imaginations, how is he to speak to us?"

My point is that God is not restricted to any particular way of speaking to us, that any human experience can be, and often is, God communicating with us. There are some special ways we hear his voice, for example in Scripture, but we perceive it also in the smile of a child, the look of love on the face of a dear friend or spouse, in nature, in science, in our thoughts.

So I want to speak a bit about using our imagination on the passages of Scripture that lend themselves to imagining. A great advantage to using our imaginations to pray is that it mostly bypasses our more rational processes, which tend to be repetitive and predictable. (We take in new information and put it into the categories we always use and the result is more like encountering ourselves than encountering the living God.)

Ignatius Loyola, whose personal experiences formed the basis of *The Spiritual Exercises*, suggests that in praying over scenes in the life of Jesus or some of his parables, we use our imagination to put ourselves into the scene and watch what is being done, listen to what is being said, and pay attention to our feelings. This is not like watching a movie where you are passive and the action is happening "out there." It's more like being in a theatrical production where you have a part in the play and where you are constantly reacting to the other actors. It requires quite an immersion in your role.

I find that when I pray this way there are roles that seem "right" for me to play. For example, I was once trying to pray the scene in John's Gospel where Jesus raises Lazarus from the dead, and I thought the part of Martha or Mary might feel right to me, but I was mistaken. I could recite their lines okay, but I had no feeling for what I was saying or doing. So I tried being one of the crowd who complained that Jesus could have come earlier and prevented his good friend's death, but I couldn't get into that part either. Well, the field was narrowing to either taking Jesus' part or Lazarus', and Lazarus didn't have much interesting to say, so I tried Jesus and again it didn't feel right.

Reluctantly I got into the tomb and lay down on the cold slab and felt the wrappings around me binding me, and I felt the absence of life. It felt cold, dark, and isolated, as though there were no future, no energy. And with reluctance I felt this was exactly where I belonged. Cue Jesus with his "Lazarus come forth" and I could feel something in me start to come alive that had been dead for a long time. It took days before I had a name for the feeling and it turned out to be hope. I had no idea there was something important in me that had died but once the Lord called it forth I knew it had been dead.

Frequently, people who pray that the Lord heal something in them discover something they didn't even know was wounded (or worse, dead) until it's healed and restored to life. I need to caution you, if you pray this way, the scene doesn't always evolve the way it's recorded in Scripture. I remember praying the scene of the Woman at the Well where I seemed to fit the part of the woman. Really wanting to do it "right," I lowered the bucket down into the water and started cranking the handle to raise it, when the figure of Jesus said to me, "Do you really want to fool with that bucket or would you like to talk?" At that point I forgot the bucket. I could not hide from his tender gaze that touched and revealed what felt most vulnerable within me. In this intimate exchange, Jesus revealed not only a glimpse of himself but myself as well. The Samaritan woman experienced Jesus' non-judgmental and loving acceptance. It is an experience of being known and loved that frees us to let go of our false pretenses. Then leaving her water jar, the woman went back to the town and said to the people, "Come see a man who told me everything I ever did."

My wife has a look she gives me which she describes as not looking at me but looking in me. It reminds me of the line in the movie "I See You." When she gives me that look it makes me uncomfortable, like I'm being stripped naked on the spot and all my layers of persona and pretense are pierced. But as I yield to it I fill with tears because I know I'm being known at a deeper level than I am accustomed to and that I'm being not just accepted but loved for who I am. This is similar to the experience at the well. There is an intimate, loving, accepting communication that speaks beyond words.

Scripture References
John 11.1-46   The raising of Lazarus
John 4.1-31   The woman at the well
Mark 10.46-52   The blind beggar

Chapter Five:
The Good Son

Even if you are thoroughly familiar with the story of the Prodigal Son from Luke, please take the time now to read it through slowly (Luke 15.11-32):

"Then he said, "A man had two sons, and the younger son said to his father, 'Father, give me the share of your estate that should come to me.' So the father divided the property between them. After a few days, the younger son collected all his belongings and set off to a distant country where he squandered his inheritance on a life of dissipation. When he had freely spent everything, a severe famine struck that country, and he found himself in dire need. So he hired himself out to one of the local citizens who sent him to his farm to tend the swine. And he longed to eat his fill of the pods on which the swine fed, but nobody gave him any. Coming to his senses he thought, 'How many of my father's hired workers have more than enough food to eat, but here am I, dying from hunger. I shall get up and go to my father and I shall say to him, 'Father, I have sinned against heaven and against you. I no longer deserve to be called your son; treat me as you would treat one of your hired workers.' So he got up and went back to his father. While he was still a long way off, his father caught sight of him, and was filled with compassion. He ran to his son, embraced him and kissed him.

His son said to him, 'Father, I have sinned against heaven and against you; I no longer deserve to be called your son.' But his father ordered his servants, 'Quickly bring the finest robe and put it on him; put a ring on his finger and sandals on his feet. Take the fattened calf and slaughter it. Then let us celebrate with a feast, because this son of mine was dead, and has come to life again; he was lost, and has been found.' Then the celebration began.

Now the older son had been out in the field and, on his way back, as he neared the house, he heard the sound of music and dancing. He called one of the servants and asked what this might mean. The servant said to him, 'Your brother has returned and your father has slaughtered the fattened calf because he has him back safe and sound.' He became angry, and when he refused to enter the house, his father came out and pleaded with him.

He said to his father in reply, 'Look, all these years I served you and not once did I disobey your orders; yet you never gave me even a young goat to feast on with my friends. But when your son returns who swallowed up your property with prostitutes, for him you slaughter the fattened calf.' He said to him, 'My son, you are here with me always; everything I have is yours. But now we must celebrate and rejoice, because your brother was dead and has come to life again; he was lost and has been found.'"

The prodigal son had all he needed: a place to live, three square meals a day, and the prestige of being the son of a man of means. But he felt this longing for something more and had to leave to find it. His words to his father are cruel: Give me the share of the estate that falls to me. It's the equivalent of telling his father he wishes he were dead, but can't wait. Rather than try to stop him his father gives him the freedom to do what his son believes he must.

We're in a similar position. Our Father has given us all we need but we believe we have to search somewhere else for our happiness and fulfillment. We might leave our Father's house dramatically like the Prodigal or we may just drift away from our relationship with our Father without really noticing that we are. This is more like the Lost Sheep Syndrome than the Lost Son.

So we spend time enjoying life with what we believe are friends (keep in mind that "friends" may not always be people, but could be anything in which we invest our lives and time) and especially enjoying what seems like the freedom to do our own thing. It's like being master of our own fate and it's a heady experience. But we inevitably wind up in the pigpen or what in AA is referred to as "hitting bottom."

The truth is we're made for God and nothing short of God himself can satisfy us. As Augustine liked to phrase it: "You made us for yourself and our hearts are restless until they rest in you."

You know what this is like from your own experience. You pursue something you believe will make you happy, achieve it, and then feel empty. It's true for possessions: that car you thought would make you feel special; that job you planned would make you feel worthwhile; that praise that would make you satisfied. It's true for accomplishments. "I graduated summa cum laude and still wonder if I'm really smart; I was top salesperson in my district and still worry about my position." We're left wondering, "Is this all there is?"

What finally changes us is not that we go after something new, but that we come to our senses and realize that we're called to return to something we already had. Like Dorothy in the Wizard of Oz, we discover that there's no place like home.

In the words of the Prodigal, "Even the servants in my father's house have plenty to eat and here I am starving in this strange land." And here is the critical part. He makes a decision—I will return to my father. Now there has to be some pain in this decision. He set off confident that he could make it on his own, but now he has to eat crow to come back home. And he knows how his big brother will act. The Prodigal has even prepared a speech in which he degrades himself, not even expecting he could join the family again.

So he heads back home and the father sees him a long distance away. That says volumes about the father. He obviously has been watching and waiting for his son to return home. Those of you who are parents know this well. Your child carries a part of your own heart with them wherever they go. Jesus is telling us our Father longs for our return and watches for signs of it. (There's a beautiful line in the book of Job where he wants God to realize the consequences of destroying him. "What will you do when you yearn for me?")

However, the Prodigal's father falls on him and embraces him before he can get his "I am not worthy" speech out of his mouth. He finally mumbles something about not being worthy to be called his son, but let me be a servant in your house; and the father doesn't dignify it with a reply. Can you picture the tenderness with which the father embraces his wayward child? There's no scene of "Well, if you promise not to act so foolishly again, you can come back." There are no "well-ifs" at all.

"Get a robe and put it on him, put sandals on his feet and a ring on his finger, for this my son was lost and is found, was dead and has come back to life again." Anyone in the household can tell that this is the father's child and that he's fully restored to his place in the family. All you need to do is look at his robe, sandals, and gold ring.

But the story doesn't end on this happy note. The elder son refuses to have any part of the celebration. The father can make a fool out of himself if he wants, but he, the Good Son, won't accept his wayward brother back. But notice what the father does not say to the elder son: You shouldn't feel that way; you ought to forgive from the heart as I do. Instead he assures his boy that he's aware of all he does for the family and will have his reward. But the father can't see beyond "This my son was lost and is found, was dead and has come to life again."

Our Father is deliriously happy when we turn to him, for he has his child back: the missing part of his heart has come home. I wish I could say that there's none of me in the Elder Son and I could just identify with the Prodigal, but I can't. There's enough in me that keeps trying to "get it right" even before God and so make myself the "Good Child" of the Father and then he'll have to love me. Call it perfectionism or exaggerated independence or whatever, but it cleverly puts the burden for my being loved by the Father on my shoulders.

This presents two problems, however. One, I can never seem to get it right enough because there's always something I could have done better but didn't, and so I live in fear and with a tremendous burden to carry. And two, it's a clever way of my continuing to believe I'm completely in control of my life. When I face the fact that the Father loves me, not because I somehow earn it or deserve it, but simply because of who he is, I feel out of control and anxious. You see, there's nothing I can do to make

God have to love me but the opposite is also true: there's nothing I can do to make him stop loving me.

I suggest you take this parable of Jesus and put yourself into whatever part seems right for you and listen to what your Father has to say to **you**.

Scripture References

Luke 15.11-32	The Prodigal Son
Matthew 19.16	What must I do to possess eternal life?
Isaiah 55.2	Why spend your money on what does not satisfy?
Matthew 9.10	He ate with tax collectors and sinners.
Philippians 2.5	He emptied himself taking the likeness of a slave.

Chapter Six:
Separating Wheat from Chaff

Pray as you can, not as you can't. I think that's the most important piece of advice here. Don't try to pray like spiritual writers say they do or like someone who is in the Dark Night of the Spirit is supposed to pray, or whatever. Instead, pray what feels *real* to you at the moment. You can't meet God at any other time than now or in any other place but here. And if you feel you can't pray, make that your prayer. "Father, I want to listen to your voice not my own monotonous one, but I don't know how to do that," and so on. The content is irrelevant. The connection is the key. Pray this way as long as it's genuine, as long as it's how you feel in the moment, saying what you're distracted by, what you feel you need. What won't work is putting on a "holy face" and trying to be someone other than who you are **right now**. Your Father doesn't need you to appear good and holy; he already knows you're good and holy; you're the one in the dark about how that would even look, so you won't pull it off anyway.

What sometimes helps me is a prayer such as "I can't get to where you are (because I don't even know where that is), so I need you to be where I am." Invite the Lord into your messy house. That's where he feels most at home.

When you pray and mind chatter intrudes, such as "Am I doing this right?" Or "Why would God pay attention to me?" Or "Wow, that was a powerful experience of God—maybe I'm somebody special! I wonder whether other people who make retreats have such profound experiences as I do." You get the idea. Don't try not to think these thoughts. That effort will only make them stronger and you can't stop them without thinking them. Just ask the Father to not let your "stuff" get in the way of the relationship between the two of you. Tell him how important that relationship is to you.

All right, now you may be thinking, "I'm silent and listening but how do I know which thoughts, emotions, and directives are from God and not just me talking to myself?" That's the question of discernment: How do I filter all the words so that I can trust that what I'm hearing is genuinely God's voice?

The ultimate way of knowing what is of God and what is not is the outcome of following that voice in your own life. "By their fruits you shall know them." But it's nearly impossible to live, discerning what is God's voice and what is not by waiting to see what results we get. That's like trying to live with a life partner to whom you will only commit when you see everything they tell you produce the results they promised. A relationship is based on trust. Every relationship. Eventually you know the person well enough that you trust what they say and you have enough experience to know when they're being sincere with you.

So it is when listening for God's voice. After a time you will recognize the sound of his voice or the way it affects you and you will trust him enough that you're free to act on it.

We've been talking about listening to the voice of God, but how do you distinguish your own voice from the voice of God? Maybe what you're hearing in your mind and experiencing in your feelings are just wishful thinking? Here are some signs that people find helpful in discerning the voice of God from their own inner voice:

First, what the voice of God says is too good to be true. It's so different from what you have been telling yourself that it surprises you and the content is beyond what you could have imagined. A friend used to tell me "God is the God of a Big Surprise." I owe you an example. I was making a retreat and had done all the "praying" I set for myself for the day, so I was just relaxing by taking a walk when I was impressed by the setting sun, how large it appeared. And I felt something inside me around chest level that was like an affirmation of my existence; it was as though the sun and I were connected and the sun was glad I was here. I was moved to tears by the experience and when I tried to put words to it this is what came out: "I have spoken you like a word that will never be unsaid."

Surprise? Suns had never spoken to me before or made me cry. Too good to be true? I work so hard to be a "good" person and here my goodness was affirmed as just pure gift without my "doing" anything at all and it wasn't anything that I earned! That experience changed something basic in the way I regarded myself and upset the way I assumed life is lived—namely that one "earns" one's value.

Second, when God speaks, the experience is one of peace not of confusion. That doesn't mean it's just what we wanted to hear; sometimes what he tells us is very challenging. But despite that there is no turmoil about it. God is not a God of confusion. When it's God's word we're hearing, it's not like a command that we are then to go out and obey as best we can. His word brings with it the ability to act, it gives us a freedom and capacity that we didn't have before. Hence the sense of peace.

Checking your voice of God against the beliefs of your Christian community is also a valuable aid to discernment. If what you are hearing conflicts dramatically with what your fellow Christians believe, you should probably be cautious about giving it credence.

Taking the matter of discernment from the opposite side, what are some indications of an experience that may look as though it came from God but likely didn't? One of these signs is that the voice we hear is repetitious, obsessive, and boring. It's really the other side of the coin of my first suggestion, that God's voice brings something new. I had the experience of the recurring thought that I ought to be doing more for the poor which seemed like the sort of message God would send, but the effect of the message was to make me feel less acceptable to my Father and more likely to dodge prayer opportunities because I felt so guilty. And the message was the same over and over again but without any experience of a new capacity to act on it. In fact it depleted my energy and put more burden on me to do something. Guilt is great when it moves us to make needed changes in our lives, but when it's not Good News but Old Advice, it's not likely that it is God's voice we're listening to.

One final suggestion about discerning whose voice we are hearing that fits the "not-from-God" category is that people who are basically living a moral Christian life are more likely to be misled by religious experiences that encourage them to pile on more and more obligations to do good things, until they become unable to bear the burden and they give up in disgust. If you can find an experienced spiritual director you can work with, the help it will give you in "separating wheat from chaff" is incalculable.

Scripture References

Romans 8.26   The Holy Spirit prays in us

John 10.2-5   The sheep listen to his voice

1 Kings 19.11-13   And after the fire came a gentle whisper

Chapter Seven:
Do You Want to Be Healed?

There are many aspects of Jesus' life that are worth focusing our attention on and each seems to bring with it a grace, an insight, an understanding, a movement within us that both puts us in touch with our own humanity and with the plan the Father has for us in certain areas of our lives.

In the Gospel narratives, seventy-five percent of the passages are stories of healing. The impression I get from the Gospels is of a Jesus who is intensely concerned with teaching and healing. He went about with a certain urgency telling people about God and freeing people from illnesses so they could get on with living life to the fullest. After Jesus' time this came to be called the Good News. While the people he healed recovered physical health they also experienced an interior healing; something within was unlocked or set free. We could look on Jesus' patients as people who realized, because of their illness, that they were caught, stuck, unable to walk or see, unable to hear or live at peace with others, unable to stand upright or mix with the rest of humanity. And many of those had known their illness for years, some for a lifetime.

While we can't put ourselves physically along the paths Jesus walked and hope for his healing touch, we can put ourselves on those paths in our imagination and experience the interior healing that people in his day experienced. I'd like to lay out for you some of Jesus' healings and invite you to put yourself into whichever of these scenes calls out to you. My own experience of praying this way is that I've come to know three things: how stuck I am (I'm ill), how willing Jesus is to unstick me, and how free I sometimes become because of his healing touch.

Later, on the occasion of a Jewish feast, Jesus went up to Jerusalem. Now in Jerusalem by the Sheep Pool, there is a place with the Hebrew name Bethesda. Its five porticoes were crowded with sick people lying there blind, lame or otherwise disabled. There was one man who had been sick for thirty-eight years. Jesus, who knew this man had been sick a long time, said when he saw him lying there, "Do you want to be healed?" "Sir," the sick man answered, "I do not have anyone to plunge me into the pool once the water has been stirred up. By the time I get there, someone else has gone in ahead of me." Jesus said to him, "Stand up! Pick up your mat and walk!" The man was immediately cured; he picked up his mat and began to walk. Later on Jesus found him in the temple precincts and said to him, "Remember, now, you have been cured. Give up your sins so that something worse may not overtake you." (John 5.6-9,14)

This is a case where the person had been ill for a very long time, 38 years, John tells us. We aren't told what his sickness was. Possibly he was lame since Jesus tells him to walk and since he had a difficult time getting into the pool. But several things strike me. First, Jesus went after the sick man; the initiative was Jesus'. We don't have any indication the man even knew who Jesus was or that Jesus could heal; and he was not aware of his desire to be whole. When Jesus initiates a conversation with him by asking, "Do you want to be made well?" the man doesn't even answer the question! Instead he focuses on the obstacles to doing anything different from what he's been doing for 38 years. He tells Jesus all the reasons why he can't be healed.

Can I relate to this one! Sometimes I've lived with my lack of freedom for so long that I don't even notice it. I've become comfortable with being stuck, even to the point of fearing that if I weren't stuck, I wonder who I would be. Then when this is called to my attention, I zero in on why it couldn't be any other way. One of the blessings of marriage is having someone who can let you know where you're stuck and being able to argue with that spouse over why you couldn't possibly change.

Early in my work as a therapist I thought my clients would be grateful if I told them what was causing their problems and they'd be eager for me to tell them how to solve them. In a few cases, that's true, but not generally. First, they often wouldn't come back if I told them what was causing their problems; and if they did we had long conversations about why their parents made them this way, why their wife or husband forced them to be this way, why they were too old to be any other way, and so on. Sometimes people just need to talk about their predicament before they're ready to do something about it; and other times they're testing me to see whether I can be trusted to accept them as they reveal parts of themselves they're ashamed of.

But here Jesus is seeking out the sick man, not even able to get a "yes" to his question, "Do you want to be healed?" and then healing him anyway. There's hope for me still! If it fits, put yourself into that scene and perhaps be the person who can't get it together to get on with your life.

Here's another scene in Luke 18.35-43:

"As he drew near Jericho, a blind man sat at the side of the road begging. Hearing a crowd go by the man asked, "What is that?" The answer came that Jesus of Nazareth was passing by. He shouted out, "Jesus, Son of David, have pity on me!" Those in the front sternly ordered him to be quiet, but he cried out all the more, "Son of David, have pity on me!" Jesus halted and ordered that he be brought to him. "What do you want me to do for you?" "Lord," he answered, "I want to see." Jesus said to him, "Receive your sight. Your faith has healed you." At that very moment he was given his sight and began to follow him, giving God the glory. All the people witnessed it and they too gave praise to God."

This healing is different in several ways. First, the blind man knew perfectly well that he wanted to see and that Jesus was famous for curing the sick. He took the initiative in getting Jesus' attention and was willing to overcome the resistance of the sensible people who tried to shut him up. Who are those people in front sternly ordering him to be quiet? Maybe they are people who "know" how things ought to be done, or people who have a difficult time with disorder. They may be the type who wants everybody to take a number. You know, I have to admit I see some of me in these folks. I want the kingdom of God to come but in an orderly, dignified way. Here's someone who really knows his problem and is determined to get what he needs from Jesus. What I love about this healing is Jesus' question. Here's a blind man standing before him who's been screaming for mercy and Jesus asks, "What do you want me to do for you?" In this case Jesus apparently wants to hear the obvious from the blind man: I want to see!

This, I find, is a good contemplation when I think I'm clear about where I'm stuck and I need to beg Jesus to heal me. But it's also a good one when I just can't see what to do next and I need sight.

You may want to be the blind man before Jesus and ask him what you can't see. Or what is keeping you from seeing. Or, skip the preliminaries and just open your eyes. You sometimes don't know what you can't see until you see it.

Here's a third healing in Mark 9.14-27:

"And one of the crowd answered him, 'Teacher, I brought you my son, possessed with a spirit which makes him mute; and whenever it seizes him, it slams him to the ground and he foams at the mouth, and grinds his teeth and stiffens out. I told your disciples to cast it out, and they could not do it.' And He answered them and said, 'O unbelieving generation, how long shall I be with you? How long shall I put up with you? Bring him to me!' They brought the boy to him. When he saw him, immediately the spirit threw him into a convulsion, and falling to the ground, he began rolling around and foaming at the mouth. And He asked his father, 'How long has this been happening to him?' And he said, 'From childhood. It has often thrown him both into the fire and into the water to destroy him. But if you can do anything, take pity on us and help us!' And Jesus said to him, 'If you can?' All things are possible to him who believes." Immediately the boy's father cried out and said, 'I do believe; help my unbelief.'

When Jesus saw that a crowd was rapidly gathering, He rebuked the unclean spirit, saying to it, 'You deaf and mute spirit, I command you, come out of him and do not enter him again.'

After crying out and throwing him into terrible convulsions, it came out; and the boy became so much like a corpse that most of them said, 'He is dead!' But Jesus took him by the hand and raised him; and he got up."

The reason I chose this healing miracle is for those of us who think we never do it right enough. We don't believe well enough. We don't trust enough. We don't pray enough. We aren't kind enough. We don't live the Christian life we should. We don't say our morning and evening prayers. We are the people who make retreats because we hope this will help us to "get it right." I'm not saying there's anything wrong with striving to do all these things. But it's a problem if our shortcomings and sins are allowed to stand *between* us and our loving God rather than bringing us *to* him to ask for what we need. It's like waiting to go to the doctor until we feel better. This way of thinking can be an excuse for keeping the Lord at a distance from us since we know that "Lord, I am not worthy." This thinking also can keep us from opening our hearts to the love the Father wants to pour into us. And it can keep us focused on ourselves and our inadequacies rather than on Jesus who brings life in abundance for free.

Let me give you an example. I've heard it said and I've said, "I don't know if I have strong enough faith to get through this." Here the emphasis is in the wrong place. It's not a matter of me having enough faith. I don't rely on my faith but on God. It's God who is my rock, my strength, my fortress, and my salvation. Not my faith in God. My faith waxes and wanes, but it isn't my anchor. God is. And I'm not so powerful that I can put my lack of faith between him and me; he comes right through my various limitations and heals whatever in me needs his healing balm.

I encourage you to take any of these healings of Jesus as a setting to be with him and let him do what he desires to do for you. But feel free to take any other setting as a place for you and him to meet.

P.S. Even if you can't seem to get the focus off yourself, he'll still give you what you need.

Scripture References

John 5.14	By the sheep pool
Luke 18. 35-43	The blind man near Jericho
Mark 9.17-27	Help the little faith I have
Luke 13.10	The woman who couldn't stand up straight
Luke 7.1	I am not worthy for you to enter my house.
Luke 5.12	Touching a leper
Luke 5.17	Paralyzed man through the roof
Mark 5.12	Daughter of Jairus and the woman with a hemorrhage

Chapter Eight:
The Passion: Were You There?

When we come to consider Jesus' passion, it's like meeting something we're very familiar with as well as something we would rather not be in touch with. We know the suffering Jesus because we see ourselves in him, but it's a part of ourselves we'd most like to avoid. From the point of view of the Jewish establishment, Jesus had to be gotten out of their lives. They hated the Romans who ruled them but at least they had learned to live with them. If this Jesus were allowed to continue to stir up the people, the Romans might well crush their political compromise and destroy their nation. They had done it in other nations within memory. "The Romans will take away our authority."

After the last supper with his friends Jesus goes across the Kedron River to a garden that he and his disciples used to frequent and he takes with him Peter, James, and John (the ones he showed himself to in his Transfiguration) to pray. His mood deteriorates from the feelings of closeness and connection at the last supper, to his feeling troubled and distressed. And he asks the three to come apart and watch with him while he goes off a bit to pray. His prayer is, "Don't make me go through this." And he ends with, "Not my will but yours."

Don't jump to "not my will" too quickly. I think it's important to spend some time with "Don't make me go through this." Did the Father will Jesus to die? Did he take any kind of pleasure at the suffering of his beloved son? So what was this will of the Father for Jesus? It was to be true to what he came for, to bring life in abundance, to save what was in danger of being lost. If he continued to do that will, he was going to die for it. What was his alternative? To just walk away and forget the business he was about? To return to Nazareth and do a little carpentry? To abandon his disciples who had come to believe in him? The Father takes no pleasure in any of our suffering. Jesus didn't die to prove that he loves us; he loved and loves us so much that he was willing to die for us.

When he returns to the three disciples, he finds them asleep. They know something terrible is on the way and their sense of self-preservation tries to keep them out of it. Jesus is looking for some connection with his friends, some feeling of belonging; but his friends are just not up to it.

After his arrest, Jesus is brought before the religious leaders of his own people and they cast about for some justifications for getting rid of him. They say he subverts the people. (Translation: He upsets the order of things, which we hate, but at least we're familiar with it.) He heals on the Sabbath. (Translation: We've got laws that keep us safe from God's wrath and he won't abide by them.) He said he'd destroy our temple. (Translation: The holy place where we can keep God out of daily life and in a safe place means nothing to him.) It's clear the decision has already been made: This guy has got to go; all that remains are the details of how to justify it. What they're looking for is a story that makes it okay to do what they've already decided to do. Isn't that familiar?

You remember the scene before Pilate where the structure of Roman law might have saved Jesus from the hatred of the Scribes and Pharisees, but where Pilate's fear of losing his power makes him hand Jesus over to the crowd. But before he does he has Jesus scourged, believing that the sight of his broken body might move the crowd to pity. A Roman scourging was a brutal business. The person was tied to a low pillar, stripped, and then lashed with a whip that had multiple strands to it. Embedded in the tips of the strands were pieces of metal or bone designed to tear the flesh as they lashed across the back. Then the soldiers whipped the person as hard as they could with 40 lashes minus one. I recall the musical Jesus Christ Superstar in which the scourging is represented by a repetitive musical background while the lashes are counted out one by one. I felt the hitting would never stop and I wasn't the one being struck!

On a recent retreat, I was using my imagination to witness Jesus being scourged and thinking how brutal this was; how could a human being do this to one just like himself, when the soldier handed the whip to me and said, "Finish the job." To my disgust I took up scourging Jesus where the soldier had left off. It was a powerful and uncomfortable experience and I left it wondering what evil in me could do such a thing. The scene stayed with me for a couple of days during which my retreat seemed to go nowhere. I felt bored with the silence and considered leaving the retreat early. I was reading through Mark's gospel and began noticing how often he has Jesus say, "Wake up" or "What I say to you I say to all, 'Wake up!'" And it began to dawn on me that the "evil" in me that could scourge Jesus was my condition of not being awake and that the body of Jesus I have been whipping is his now-body (we sometimes call it his Mystical Body)—my fellow humans. The people I tear the flesh of are the people in my life and the people I'm careful to keep out of my life. First my wife and when, for example, I do my chores but let her carry the burden of all the unexpected things that need doing and when I do help, I regard this as "working on her projects." Basically not taking responsibility. I don't do this deliberately but I'm not awake. Then I saw how it expanded to the folks in my neighborhood to whom I could reach out. But the condition that hurt the most was my awareness of the poor in my own city who I never have to see because I live in a "nice" neighborhood that doesn't make me drive through "those areas."

Finally they get Jesus to Calvary, strip him, and nail him to the cross, which they haul up for everyone to see. Now it's perfectly clear that we intend to get Jesus out of our world once and for all. We're doing our best as humans to put God to death. It's humanity at our worst. Here the evil that lurks beneath the surface of our little sins comes out in the open. And it's met with "Father forgive them, for they don't know what they are doing." What an incredible surprise! When we're doing our worst we're met with forgiveness. We don't get any more sinful than this; we don't try any harder to live our lives *our* way and independent of God than this. And right here we meet the embrace of the Father and his forgiveness.

"For one will hardly die for a righteous man; though perhaps for the good .man someone would dare even to die. But God demonstrates his own love toward us, in that while we were yet sinners, Christ died for us. Much more then, having now been justified by his blood, we shall be saved from the wrath of God through him." (Romans 5.7-9)

There is something incredibly healing about coming before the crucified Jesus. Looking on the crucified Jesus has the power to put our lives back in perspective. The things we fill our lives with take on less importance; our distorted values get straightened. Before the crucified, that big screen TV I've been wanting loses its urgency; the house I'm going to buy to impress my friends pales; the fact that my wife doesn't see things my way becomes less significant; the fact that my kids don't want to go to church anymore feels less like a crisis to me. You fill in the blanks.

"He was despised and forsaken of men,
 A man of sorrows and acquainted with grief;
 And like one from whom men hide their face
 He was despised, and we did not esteem him.
 Surely our griefs he himself bore,
 And our sorrows he carried;
 Yet we ourselves esteemed him stricken,
 Smitten of God, and afflicted.
 But he was pierced through for our transgressions,
 He was crushed for our iniquities;
 The chastening for our wellbeing fell upon him,
 And by His stripes we are healed." (Isaiah 53.3-5)

Most good people don't set out to lose their connection with God; it's just something that happens while we're busy with the ten thousand tasks of life.

"All of us, like sheep, have gone astray,
 Each of us has turned to his own way;
 But the LORD has caused the iniquity of us all
 To fall on him." (Isaiah 53.6)

Jesus crucified is especially healing for us when we are grieving a loss. Blessed are those who mourn for they will be comforted. When we suffer loss there's a feeling of being abandoned by God or punished by God, or at least a feeling of not being loved enough by God. Seeing his son crucified shakes that fear. There's nobody the Father loved more than his son Jesus and look at what he endured. He who did not spare His own Son, but delivered him over for us all, how will he not also with him freely give us all things?   Is there anything the Father will deny us given what he has already handed over?

Scripture References

Isaiah 53.3	Like one from whom people hide their face
Matt 20.18-19	They will condemn him to death
Luke 22.44	His sweat became like drops of blood
Galatians 6.14	The world is crucified to me and I to the world
Isaiah 53.4-5	By his stripes we are healed.
Revelation 7.14	Washed their garments white in the blood of the Lamb

Chapter Nine:
Resurrection

Can you imagine what it was like for Jesus when he finally died and realized fully what he had done for us? Now he could see from the Father's own perspective what a profound effect his life and death had on the world. It certainly seems that he was unaware of this when he shouted out to know why God had abandoned him. Now his ministry and teaching, his work with his disciples, his healing the sick, the opposition of the religious leaders, his leaving behind anything he could depend on except the Father, all made sense to him in a way they couldn't before.

I'm sure you've had the experience of thinking that some event in your life was the end of everything good. And later you look back at it and see what life has come to you because of it. We only clearly know the Lord's action in our lives in passover, in looking back over our shoulders. In the midst of things we can only trust that all will be well. But Jesus' work doesn't end with his death. He returns to his own, his beloved, to let them know how it turned out.

A nun told me the story of a little Vietnamese boy who was attending Catholic school for the first day, and all the kids were brought into church for the start of the day. It happened that the parish had a very realistic crucifix over the altar that depicted Jesus in graphic detail and when the boy saw it he cried out "What happened?" As the teachers rushed over to comfort him another boy told him "It's all right, he gets out okay at the end!"

Now, Jesus' ministry becomes one of consoling those who had hoped he was going to be the one who would set Israel free. Not only were their hopes crushed that he would be the messiah, but each of them had deserted him when he had the most need of their support. So they were dealing with disappointment (some of them had left everything to follow him); fear that the same thing might happen to them that happened to Jesus; and guilt that they had abandoned their friend in his hour of greatest need. You can imagine them asking, "*What do we do now?*" When he was with them they had a sense of direction. He seemed to know what he was doing and what they should do as well. They had come to depend on his presence. Now all that was gone. In his public life he had tried to prepare them for what was coming. He had shown himself to Peter, James and John at the Transfiguration when he shone bright as the sun. He told them many times that the Son of Man must be put to death by the scribes and Pharisees and rise from the dead. Remember how they discussed among themselves what "rise from the dead" might mean?

After three days he begins appearing to them alive. But he's different now and at first they don't recognize him. In John 20.11-18, Mary Magdalene and the other Mary find the tomb empty with the stone rolled back; Mary sees Jesus in the garden there but mistakes him for the gardener. Only when he calls her by her name does she recognize him. The women run back to the disciples who are locked up in a room together and tell them about the empty tomb and Peter and John have a foot race, (which John wins, he tells us), to the tomb and they find it just as the women had said, but Jesus they did not find.

While they're all still locked up, Jesus shows up in the middle of his disciples. (Sometimes I don't know how to get to the Lord and my prayer is often, "I'm locked up, please show up in the middle of me since I don't know how to get to you.") He doesn't knock at their door; simply put, he wasn't there one minute and the next he is. He initiates the conversation with "Peace be with you." Well, if they weren't scared to death before, they are now. They think they're seeing a ghost and are highly agitated. If I had them in my counseling office I would diagnose them as having trauma-induced anxiety disorders. Jesus seems to know exactly what they're thinking so he says again, "Peace be with you. I'm not a ghost." Then he shows them his wounds, invites them to touch him, and finally asks them for something to eat. Ghosts, at least, don't eat. And they give him a piece of baked fish. By this time their fear, confusion, and guilt are forgotten and they're happy to see him again.

Two of his disciples have left Jerusalem that day and are on their way to Emmaus when Jesus catches up with them and asks what they're so animatedly talking about. (Luke 24.13) They don't recognize him. The "not recognizing Jesus" theme recurs throughout the time after his resurrection, and I believe it has significance for us who are all living in the post-resurrection time. Jesus is not as evident now as he was when he walked among us. So the disciples explain all that has happened to Jesus of Nazareth these past three days and how they were hoping that he would be the one who would set Israel free. There's something touching about the phrase "we were hoping." How they thought things would work out isn't at all how they do. Their dreams have been wiped out and they're dejected.

We can certainly identify with that experience. The way we planned our lives to go, the way we expected our marriage to work out, the hopes we had for our children—all those "we had hoped" moments of awareness in our own lives. This may be a good place to talk with the Lord about those disappointments.

He clearly wants to hear about them. Look at how he deals with the two disciples; he lets them pour their hearts out to him.

Then Jesus opens to them the Scriptures about himself making it clear that all these things **must** have happened. What Jesus is doing is revealing his own new understanding of why all this had to be and he is sharing it with his friends so that all this has a place to rest within them. Think back on some of the awful things that have happened in your own life and maybe you're far enough removed from them now to see that your life didn't end in death but in new life. And if you're in the middle of some of them, ask the risen Lord to enable you to share this with him.

You recall the details, how Jesus acts like he's leaving them and they beg him to stay and have supper with them. And how they recognize him in the Breaking of the Bread. It's a flash-forward to the early Christian community who experienced him present in their Breaking of the Bread. And it's still the place where we continue to recognize him in the Eucharist.

It makes "sense" to them now. It's the sort of thing we expect to happen when we encounter Jesus face-to-face when we die. And the sort of thing we may catch glimpses of in our present life. Oh, that's why that happened the way it did!

The result is their hearts are burning within them as hope is born anew from the ashes of despair. That "burning within them" is important because that is the gift of the Holy Spirit. The burning leads to action: they get up and return to Jerusalem where it's not safe to be one of his followers. It isn't "just a feeling" although that's how they are aware of it. It's a new ability they didn't have before. We might call it "courage."

The Jesus the early Christian community experienced was not a resuscitated Jesus, like Lazarus whom Jesus brought back to life only for him to eventually die again, but a Jesus who was different, who was Lord and who had become a "life-giving spirit." And this is the Jesus we experience in our own lives today. We experience him enabling us to do things we could not before and we have the capacity to do them. The Jesus we continue to meet in the healing miracles from the Gospels, for example, is not a Jesus from 2,000 years ago, but one who is alive and active in us now. That bears repeating: the resurrected Jesus is someone who is alive and active in us *now*.

That's why it's not wise to use retreat time to give ourselves lectures on what we should be doing, but better to ask and wait on the Lord to give us, not a command, but the ability to do what we can. That ability is the Holy Spirit. Sometimes She (the Spirit always seems feminine to me) comes to us as a burning within that fires us into action. At other times She's the courage to act that we didn't have before, or She's a gift of wisdom to know when and how to act. But always, She's a gift of peace even in the midst of struggles.

We as church are always getting glimpses of the Lord in our world and then seeing him disappear. It's as if we experience God showing himself to us in glimpses through the events of life and then remaining hidden. Only now, we have the gift of the Holy Spirit poured out into our hearts to guide, comfort, enlighten, and encourage us on our journey. For after his resurrection Jesus sent us this indwelling gift so we wouldn't be left orphans.

As you spend some time with the scenes of Jesus' consoling ministry and making sense of things to his friends after he rose from the dead, I suggest that you allow Jesus to console you and renew your own hope that those things you can't make sense of in your own life will bring you to where you need to be to receive your own new life. "And pray in the confidence that the Holy Spirit prays within you sometimes in sighs and groans too deep for words." (Romans 8.26)

Scripture References

John 20.11-18	Mary Magdalene doesn't recognize Jesus
John 20.1-10	The stone rolled back, foot race to the tomb
Luke 24.13	I am not a ghost
Luke 24.36-49	The road to Emmaus

Chapter Ten:
For the God Who Has Everything

In *The Spiritual Exercises*, (translation of the *Exercises*, Louis J. Puhl, S.J., 1951) St. Ignatius is mindful of the art of gift-giving, so at the end of a retreat he suggests we look back at what we have been given by the Father through his son Jesus and ask ourselves what can we give back to him. "What return can I make to the Lord for all he has given me? I will take the cup of salvation and call upon the name of the Lord." (Psalm 116.12)

With people we can give something they don't already have, but what do you give a God who has everything? Besides, what do we have that he could possibly lack? Everything we could think of offering is already his to begin with.

Well, there is something. The Lord has decided to keep his hands off our freedom. He won't do anything to force us to do something. So respectful is he of our freedom that he'll allow us to lose our very selves if we so choose. Many spiritual writers have suggested that the reason the Lord hides himself from us and only shows himself by glimpses is that if we saw him as he is, we'd be so overwhelmed with joy and fall so in love with him that we'd have no choice but to prefer him over everything. But that wouldn't be love; it would be necessity. In the Old Testament we frequently encounter the statement, "No one can see the face of God and live." But he asks for our love not our servitude, and someone who has to love can't really love at all. They can't help themselves. Jesus said to his disciples, "I don't call you slaves for a slave doesn't know what his master is doing, but I call you friends because I have told you everything I am doing."

So the one thing we have that the Lord doesn't have is our freedom. And to give him the gift of our freedom is to love him freely, and that's exactly what he hopes for from us.

One way to enter into this gift-exchange is to recall the gifts he has given you, so I suggest you spend some time reviewing your gifts. You might start big with the universe that's so incredibly huge and beautiful and violent all at the same time. As we look off in all directions, we find galaxies, stars, worlds, and moons in the billions; and we get some small insight into how the Lord made the heavens and the earth. We can see back nearly 14 billion years into space and time and see how everything created is rushing out from a central point of creation and expanding at an ever-increasing rate. We've just recently become able to see planets around other stars like our own and wonder if there's someone *there* wondering whether we're *here*. We've been given a home planet that is in the "Goldilocks" distance from our sun, that is, "not too hot and not too cold" for us to live. Of all the universes that could have been, this one is set up for the evolution of intelligent life. Someone planned our garden for us with great care.

Take your reflections closer to home and look at the place where you live through no merit on your part. Look at the communities you are a member of—a society, a nation, a civilization, a Church, a family—and see how the Lord is loving you so generously and giving you so much, not of things but of his own goodness. It's as though he can't help but shower gifts on you.

Spend some time looking at the world you are in—*here*. Go for a walk and let the goodness of the earth—the trunks of the trees, the grass, the birds, the sky—all speak to you of him who is loving you by delighting your senses everywhere you look and listen.

Look more deeply at the graces he's given you during this retreat: the grace of being able to come aside for a few days and spend time with him alone. You may be well aware how many people couldn't pull that off. Reflect on whatever healing you have experienced at his hands, whatever hope he has given you in painful situations, whatever courage he gives you to continue your walk through life with him.

And it's not just that he gives you things; he is in the things he gives you. When you taste delicious food or drink, he's delighting you through those things. Ignatius uses the expression, "God, as it were, labors to delight and sustain us through the things he has made." How much more is God laboring to delight and sustain you through other people, family, friends, mentors, and children? Look into a child's eyes to see God looking back at you with love. Look into the eyes of a spouse or good friend and see God accepting you just as you are. Recall that loving look of someone who simply loves you and know that God is looking out at you through those eyes, admiring you, pleased to have made you in his own image and likeness.

And then you may want to visualize all that is good, that is lovely, that is holy, that is exciting, that is life-giving flowing out from God the way light flows out from a bright light, one so bright you can't really look at it directly but have to look away at the gifts flowing out from it. The idea here is that everything is a message of love and acceptance and affirmation. Paul came to understand this: "For I am convinced that neither death, nor life, nor angels, nor principalities, nor things present, nor things to come, nor powers, nor height, nor depth, nor any other created thing, will be able to separate us from the love of God, which is in Christ Jesus our Lord." (Romans 8.38)

You might wish to imagine a powerful river of goodness rushing out from its source, or a source of intense light that you can't look at directly, but which makes everything bright and full of life. If you've seen the Hubble Space Telescope images of a pillar of dust in space giving birth to new stars and a powerful source of light off to one side illuminating this incredible event, you might use that image to help your imagination.

It's not important how you do this contemplation; the point is to be with whatever gives you life right now and recognize where that life keeps coming from. And you might want to use Ignatius' prayer of thanksgiving called his Suscipe (Take and Receive):

"Take, Lord, and receive all my liberty,
my memory, my understanding
and my entire will,
All I have and call my own.
You have given all to me.
To you, Lord, I return it.
Everything is yours; do with it what you will.
Give me only your love and your grace.
That is enough for me."

Scripture References

Psalm 116.12	What return can I make to the Lord?
Romans 8.38	Neither height nor depth
Genesis 2.2	God rested from all this labors
Psalm 8.4	Your heavens, the work of your fingers
Psalm 145	God in all his works
1 Timothy 6.16	God dwells in unapproachable light
Psalm 4.6	Let the light of your face shine on us
1 John 1.5	God is light; in him there is no darkness.

About the Author

Educator, psychotherapist, and seasoned spiritual director, Richard Stoltz held degrees in theology, spirituality, physics and counseling. He was a Jesuit for more than thirty years teaching, preaching and directing retreats throughout the country.

Richard recognized the voice of God in his life, heard in the gentleness of silence and lived in the joy of loving and being loved. He lived that love both in the Sacrament of Holy Orders and, later, in the Sacrament of Matrimony. He and his wife Maureen continued God's ministry in teaching, counseling and in spiritual direction and preached retreats. In this book, Richard shares his humanness, gentleness and his own intimacy with God, offering us a glimpse of God and ourselves.

After twenty-five years of being married to his soul mate and best friend, Richard was diagnosed with metastatic pancreatic cancer and went home to God three weeks later. He embraced his dying and death with courage and deep faith knowing that he was God's Beloved.

Made in the USA
Charleston, SC
21 January 2016